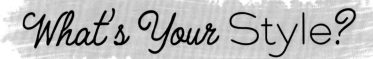

What's Your Style?

PREPPY
FASHION

KAREN LATCHANA KENNEY

⌐ Lerner Publications Company
Minneapolis

Lerner Publications Company
A division of Lerner Publishing Group, Inc.
241 First Avenue North
Minneapolis, MN 55401 U.S.A.

For reading levels and more information, look up this title at www.lernerbooks.com.

Credits: Amy Fitzgerald and Sara E. Hoffmann (editorial), Emily Harris (design), Giliane Mansfeldt (photos), Heidi Hogg (production).

Main body text set in Adrianna Light 12/14.
Typeface provided by Chank.

Library of Congress Cataloging-in-Publication Data

Kenney, Karen Latchana.
    Preppy fashion / by Karen Latchana Kenney ; illustrated by Ashley
  Newsome Kubley.
        pages   cm — (What's your style?)
    Includes index.
    ISBN 978-1-4677-1469-3 (lib. bdg. : alk. paper)
    ISBN 978-1-4677-2529-3 (eBook)
    I. Kubley, Ashley Newsome, illustrator. II. Title.
  TT507.K416825 2014
  746.9'2—dc23   2013022643

Manufactured in the United States of America
1 – PC – 12/31/13

What's Your Style?

Are *You* Preppy?

What's your favorite style? Does the clean-cut and simple look reflect your personality? Or do layered and eccentric outfits fit better with who you are? Take this quiz to find out.

1. Your perfect outfit would include
   a. cowboy boots
   b. a fitted blazer
   c. a leather jacket
   d. an ironic T-shirt

2. Who's your fashion idol?
   a. Johnny Depp
   b. Taylor Swift
   c. Miley Cyrus
   d. Vanessa Hudgens

3. Your basic, everyday shoes are
   a. combat boots
   b. boat shoes
   c. gladiator sandals
   d. splatter-painted flats

4. You keep your hair
   a. spiked and wild
   b. neat and simple
   c. neon pink
   d. messy and carefree

5. When it comes to button-down shirts, you like
   a. flannel and checked
   b. striped oxfords
   c. sports logos
   d. a military look

6. You describe your fashion personality as
   a. rough and edgy
   b. crisp and classic
   c. quirky and laid-back
   d. grungy and messy

Were your answers mostly *b*'s? If so, you're **preppy**! You like simple silhouettes and a clean look. Preppy fashion is classic. It always looks stylish and put-together.

What if you didn't have many *b*'s? No problem! Preppy fashion might not be your favorite, but you can still gain some valuable style wisdom by finding out more about this look. Let's explore what makes preppy style so timeless.

Who's Got THE LOOK?

To start learning about preppy fashion, study the stars who style themselves head-to-toe in prep wear. Each celeb puts a new twist on the look, from jewelry choices to favorite shoes.

Let's start with some really well-known preppy fashionistas—the first daughters! Their father might be the president of the United States, but when it comes to fashion, Malia and Sasha Obama are the emerging icons in their family. Malia leans more toward classic prep, while Sasha likes to mix things up with bolder color schemes and distinctive accessories. But they share a core style sense that keeps both of them looking poised and put-together on the world stage.

MALIA AND SASHA OBAMA

Malia (left) favors simple looks while Sasha (right) goes bolder with patterned pants.

How do the sisters show off their preppy style savvy? They

- wear lots of A-line skirts and printed dresses;

- love solid-color blouses, cardigans, and blazers; and

- step out in comfy yet classy ballet flats and loafers.

Check Out These Other Famous Preps!

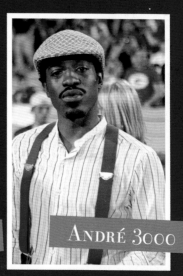

JUSTIN TIMERLAKE

JESSICA ALBA

ANDRÉ 3000

TAYLOR SWIFT

A country music superstar, Taylor Swift is known for her clean-cut and girly style. She particularly loves one preppy staple. "I'm really obsessed with oxford shoes," Taylor says. "They're my go-to comfort shoe."

That's not Taylor's only preppy style secret. She also

- keeps her silhouette simple with A-line dresses and skirts;

- has a fresh-faced look with a bold pop of red on her lips;

- pairs cute flats with cropped pants;

- loves polka dots and stripes; and

- knows how to rock a ribbon headband.

Take a peek at some of Taylor's best preppy looks.

ZAC EFRON

Tween heartthrob Zac Efron knows how to work the casual and cool preppy look. But he's also at home dressed up on the red carpet. Zac says, "I never like to look sloppy. . . . I believe I owe it to fans to be presentable when I go out."

Zac's been seen in

- a sharp and well-cut suit;

- laid-back and comfy henley sweaters;

- slim fit jeans and a crisp white T-shirt;

- a nice tie under a casual V-neck; and

- simple, sporty shoes, like Vans or Converse low tops.

Zac shows off his preppy style.

Actor Audrey Hepburn was one of the original preppy stars.

Styling Tip:

Style Icon Study

Preppy fashion has been around a long time. It was popular with famous classic style icons like Jackie Kennedy Onassis, John F. Kennedy, Grace Kelly, Audrey Hepburn, and Lauren Bacall. You can learn a lot about preppy fashion by studying their looks. Pick one style icon to study. Then find photos that show this icon's personal style. Take notes on everything, and clip photos too. You'll see certain fashion patterns appear. Use your favorites as inspiration for your own preppy look!

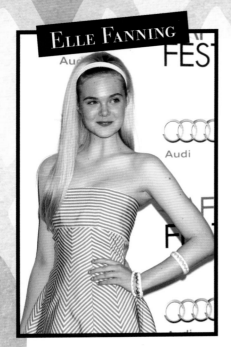

ELLE FANNING

The little sister of actress Dakota Fanning, Elle Fanning is a teen actress in her own right. She's also known for her preppy look. She is all about fashion and knows how to express her style. Elle says,

"I don't worry about what other people think about my clothes—I want to be me."

Elle shows off her classic yet unique look when she

- wears her signature A-line dresses;

- keeps her hair in place with pretty headbands;

- opts for classic color schemes, like black and white; and

- layers oxford shirts over polos for a casual look.

Do you like Elle's version of preppy chic?

How Do I
GET THE LOOK?

Where do you start when it comes to creating your own preppy wardrobe? With the basics. What are some preppy-friendly color schemes? What patterns add some fun to the style? And what cuts look more preppy than others? Some simple guidelines will help you pick out the perfect preppy essentials.

Preppy Influences

The preppy look has its roots in college prep schools and Ivy League universities from the East Coast of the United States. School uniforms inspired many preppy fashion basics—blazers, ties, button-down shirts, khakis, and loafers. Today's preppy fashionista pulls from these classic roots but also adds a modern twist.

Simple and Elegant

Think clean lines and simple silhouettes. Tailored blazers and A-line dresses work well. Simple necklines are great too, including boatnecks, scoop necks, and V-necks. If it's too flashy, stay away from it! For a true preppy look, clothes and accessories need to be modest and elegant. They also need to be well-balanced. Wear just a few layers, and keep your accessories to a minimum. And keep it natural with cotton, wool, and linen fabrics.

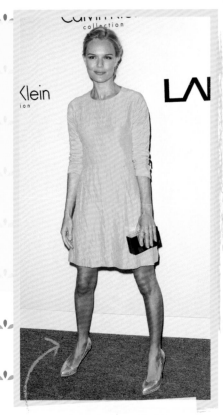

Kate Bosworth, at the 2010 Calvin Klein Collection party, shows that less is sometimes more.

Sporty and Relaxed

There's a definite sporty vibe to preppy fashion. It doesn't include your favorite baseball team's logo, though. Instead, the style echoes outfits worn for tennis, golf, boating, or lacrosse. Rugby and polo shirts, tennis skirts, and boat shoes all fit this vibe. Another popular preppy look takes its cues from horseback riding. Whether or not you're spending time in the saddle, knee-high riding boots, slim-fitting pants, and a blazer make a tasteful ensemble.

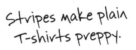

Stripes make plain T-shirts preppy.

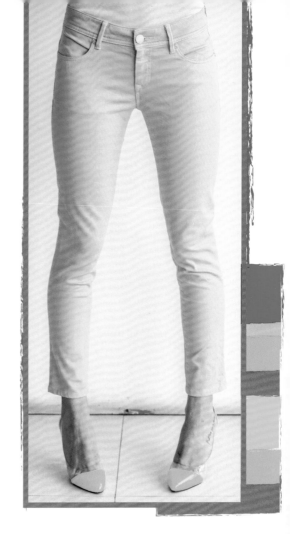

Bright Pops and Fun Patterns

The basic preppy palette includes black, white, navy, and beige. But splashes of bright colors are welcome too. Bubblegum pink, cool turquoise, neon yellow, and mint green make their way into preppy clothing. And patterns liven up the basic look. Polka dots, stripes, plaids, gingham, florals, and checks are fun for any outfit. In the summertime, you can't go wrong with madras plaid—distinctive stripes on a lightweight cotton material. And tweed is a must-have for fall and winter clothes.

You've learned the basics. So let's take a closer look at the clothing that defines true prep. It's much more than pearls and popped collars!

OXFORDS, POLOS, RUGBYS, AND CHAMBRAY

A good oxford shirt looks great on its own. It's even better when layered under a slouchy cable-knit sweater or a fitted blazer. Just make sure the collar shows. And keep it neat by tucking in your shirt. Polos and rugby shirts are great for a more casual look. Chambray shirts add a more modern twist. Try them under blazers or with brightly colored pants.

SHIFTS, A-LINES, AND PLEATS

Women's prep includes shift dresses, A-line dresses and skirts, and lots of pleats. A shift dress has a straight cut from the shoulders to the hem. A-line dresses and skirts have an A shape, getting wider at the hem. Both styles have a super-simple, clean cut. Pleated skirts come straight from the preppy roots of the school uniform. Go for a fun plaid or a pretty solid color.

Cindi Leive, editor in chief of Glamour magazine, proves that simple doesn't equal boring.

Disney Channel star Zendaya finds the fun in a colorful A-line skirt.

Pants

When it comes to pants, nothing says "preppy" like khakis and chinos. You can find both in classic tan, but patterns and colors are in style too. Go for fun plaids, wild paisleys, or vibrant colors. Nantucket Reds are a preppy staple. They're designed to fade to a salmon pink. And on the denim front, wear boot cut or skinny jeans.

French actor and fashion model Clémence Poésy favors skinny denim pants.

BLAZERS, CARDIGANS, AND SWEATERS

The right layers make the perfect preppy outfit. Go more formal with a structured blazer. You don't need to stick with navy. Try green, plaid, or even pink! For a carefree vibe, put on a cardigan. Button it up over an oxford shirt or try one over a dress. Cable-knit sweaters add a New England coastal attitude. And remember—monograms make everything preppier.

US sprinter Allyson Felix protects her preppy ensemble with a lightweight, tailored trench coat.

CLASSIC TRENCH

To keep your preppy outfits dry, you need the right coat. A trench coat is a preppy classic. Tailored and belted, it looks great over any outfit. Try the timeless navy or tan trench, or break the mold with a wilder color. You can even find trench coats in plaids.

A classic tan trench puts a preppy spin on singer and actor Ashley Walters's outfit.

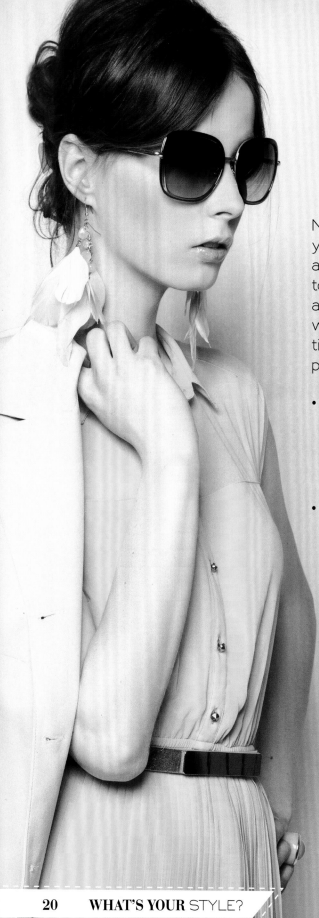

MIX & MATCH

Now you know the must-haves, but you can't just throw everything on and call it prepped. An outfit needs to be built. What do you pair with a cable-knit sweater? How do you wear a good blazer? Here are some tips for mixing and matching your preppy pieces:

- Wear a cable-knit sweater over an oxford, polo, or chambray shirt. Pair it with a cute skirt or some chic pants or jeans. You can even wear it with shorts!

- Add some plaid to your outfit. Plaid looks great on skirts, shirts, pants, blazers, shorts, or scarves. Just a touch of plaid can make any outfit look preppy.

- Balance classically elegant items with more casual pieces. Wear a blazer or a cardigan with distressed denim or faded pants.

- Search for unique pieces in thrift stores. Add these to some more traditional preppy staples, like polos or boat shoes. You can create a new spin on classic prep with your one-of-a-kind vintage items.

Preppy Blazer

You don't need an expensive blazer to look preppy. Just restyle a thrift store find with some preppy touches. Here's how.

What you need:

- a thrift store blazer (look for plaid patterns, cool checks, or fun solid colors)

- thread (in a color that matches your blazer) and a needle

- brass buttons

- a monogram patch

- safety pins

- scissors

What you do:

1. Remove the buttons from your blazer. Make sure to cut the thread carefully. You don't want to cut the blazer!

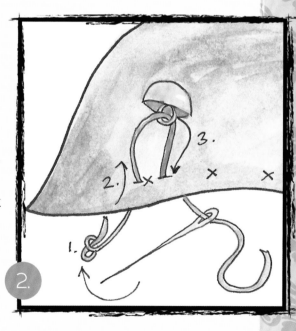

2. Sew on your brass buttons, with help from an adult if you need it. Simply go up from the inside of the blazer with the threaded needle. Go through the buttonhole and back down into the blazer. Repeat a few times for each button and knot tightly on the inside of your blazer.

3. Find the perfect spot for your patch. Pin it in place with the safety pins.

4. Sew the patch to the blazer. Use a straight stitch, which simply goes up and down through the fabric. Go all the way around the patch. Knot tightly on the inside of your blazer. Then remove the safety pins.

Try on your restyled blazer with a button-down shirt. Pretty preppy, right?

SHOES

Preppy style doesn't stop with the clothing. You need the perfect shoes as well. For a true preppy look, shoes should not go to extremes. Super high heels or really trendy kicks don't fit in. Shoot for comfortable, understated options. Here are a few of the most iconic preppy shoe styles.

OXFORDS AND LOAFERS

Oxfords are laced leather dress shoes. They started out as just a men's shoe. But there are plenty of women's styles now too. They look great with both pants and skirts. Loafers are another prep staple. And for a more girly look, try wearing them with some fun knee-high socks and a skirt. Skip the socks (or wear no-show socks) in the summer.

For special occasions, you can even find loafer-style shoes with heels!

Boat Shoes, Flip-Flops, and Sneakers

Boat shoes are a must-have for any prepster. Many are waterproof and have a white sole, making them perfect for a day offshore. Flip-flops also fit the bill. Pair them with some more formal clothing, like a blazer, for a fun and casual look. And white sneakers never go out of fashion. Match them with some patterned, colored pants.

Ballet Flats and Wedges

Some simple flats look great with dresses and skirts. Try ones with bright colors, like lemon yellow or tomato. But stay away from anything sparkly. You can look distinctive without going overboard on flashiness. Wedges are another great option for girls. Wear them with skinny pants or a skirt for a breezy summer look.

Australian model Miranda Kerr likes to wear flats when out and about in New York City.

RIDING BOOTS AND WELLIES

When you need boots, go for riding boots or wellies. Knee-high riding boots give outfits a put-together look. Wear them with skinny pants or jeans and a fitted blazer. Wellington boots, or wellies, are wet-weather boots, originally from the United Kingdom. You can find them in all kinds of colors—from bubblegum pink to hunter green. They look great with skirts, jeans, and even dresses.

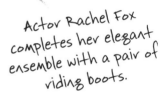

Actor Rachel Fox completes her elegant ensemble with a pair of riding boots.

Boat Shoes

Make these boat shoes from canvas slip-ons. All you need is a bit of paint and a steady hand!

What you need:

- acrylic paint in one or two colors you like

- white canvas slip-on shoes

- thin-tipped paintbrushes

What you do:

1. Pick a paint color for a line at the base of your shoes.

2. Paint a thin line around the base, just above the sole. Be careful and go slowly. You want this line to be even and straight. Repeat on the other shoe.

3. Pick a color to go on the top of the shoe. It can be the same as the base color. Or it can be a contrasting color.

4. Paint a thin line around the tongue of your shoe. If your shoe does not have a distinct tongue area, it's okay! Just paint a thin outline of the top of your shoe, starting about 1 inch (2.5 centimeters) from the edge of the shoe. Repeat on the other shoe.

5. Wait for your shoes to dry. Then match them with some linen pants. Are you ready to hit the beach?

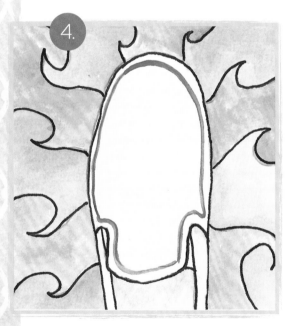

ACCESSORIES

"Simple and few" is the motto when it comes to preppy accessories. Some classy earrings or a few nautical bracelets add the right touch: not too plain, not too tacky. Here are some of the best choices to complete your preppy outfit.

HEADBANDS AND HAIR BOWS

Ribbon headbands give your hair a neat, put-together look. They're also a fun way to add color and pattern to an outfit. Find them in plaids, checks, polka dots, or stripes. You can even make your own. Add a bow to a headband for a sweet, girly look.

MEN'S WATCHES

A men's watch is big and chunky. If it's worn with a feminine outfit, it adds a fun contrast. Slip it on with a few casual bracelets for some variety.

BRACELETS

Knotted rope bracelets add a laid-back summer vibe to casual outfits. They're perfect for a day at the beach or out on a boat. Find them in cool colors, with anchor charms or anchor clasps. You can wear just one rope bracelet or layer several bracelets together. Other good bets include charm bracelets, stacks of simple gold or silver bracelets, and ribbon bracelets with button clasps.

Pearls, Pearls, Pearls

Pearls are pretty old school. But they're not just for grandmas! A simple string of pearls or a pair of pearl stud earrings will add elegance to any outfit. For a modern take, try big pearls or several strands. And don't worry if you can't afford the real thing. Imitation pearls can be just as chic!

Fedoras and Newsboys

A straw or linen fedora hat with a ribbon creates a beachy look. Flat newsboy hats are fun as well. They come in a variety of fabrics and patterns. Try a madras plaid in the summer and a warm tweed in the winter.

BOAT TOTES AND CLUTCHES

A canvas boat tote doesn't just come in handy on a boat. Smaller ones make great casual bags. Larger ones are good for day trips. And many can be monogrammed—always a nice preppy touch. For a night out, clutches are a must-have. Carry a simple quilted clutch, or try a brighter color or pattern.

Anchor Charm Bracelet

Add a nautical look to your preppy style with this easy anchor charm bracelet.

What you need:

- suede cord

- scissors

- a silver or brass-looking anchor charm with a round loop on one end

What you do:

1. Wrap the cord around your wrist about two and a half times to measure it. Then cut off that length of cord.

2. Fold your piece of cord in half. Now there should be a loop at one end. The two loose ends should be at the other end.

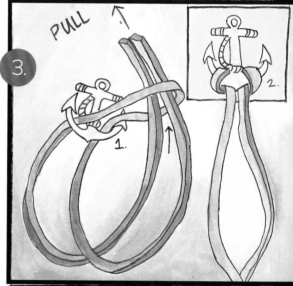

3. Put the loop around the hook end of the anchor charm. Then pull the loose ends of the cord through the loop. This will secure the loop snugly to the hooks of the anchor.

4. Cut one end of the cord at an angle. This will help it go through the metal loop on the top of the anchor charm.

5. Put the angled cord through the metal loop. Pull it through, but not tightly yet.

6. Slide the bracelet onto your wrist. Pull the cord tightly through the metal loop. Keep it loose enough so that you can take it off, though.

7. Knot the loose ends of the cord together. Then neatly trim the cord ends.

8. You're done! Now show off your new anchor bracelet with your preppiest summer outfit!

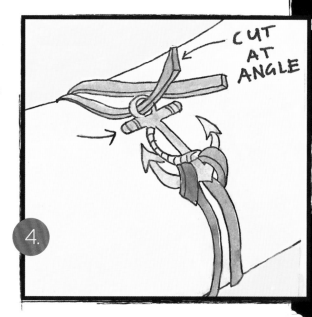

HAIR AND MAKEUP

Clean, simple, and pulled together: this is what all prepsters should aim for when it comes to personal grooming. Here are a few ways to get the right look from head to toe.

NEAT NAILS

Preppy guys and girls should have neat and clean nails. Polish should be kept simple—muted beige, pink, classic red, or clear. For a fancier occasion, a French manicure is a great treat.

Tidy and Simple Hair

Hair should also be simple and neat. No spikes or messy braids are allowed! Keep long hair in place with headbands or a ponytail. Guys often slick back their hair with pomade or wear it parted toward one side. Feel free to use hair products, but make sure your hair can still move. Aim for that beachy, breezy look, even when you're not at the beach.

Tyson Beckford (above) and Anne Hathaway (below) sport short cuts.

BLUNT AND SHORT CUTS

Keep hair looking clean and simple with blunt cuts. For girls, this often means bobs, but unlayered styles can also work for longer hair. Preppy guys usually go for short haircuts. Keep it a little longer on top, and never shave the sides. Guys should also stay away from too much facial hair. It can look messy and ungroomed.

Willow Smith rocks a blunt cut.

Natural Makeup

Like the rest of your style, makeup should be simple and clean-looking. Never use too much makeup. You want a fresh face and a healthful glow. Try some mineral foundation and a bronzer. For the eyes, go with a natural-looking eye shadow and a brush of mascara. On your lips, choose a subtle pink gloss. Once in a while, though, you may want a bolder look. If your parents sign off on it, red lipstick is great for a night out.

Carey Mulligan keeps her makeup looking natural.

Grosgrain Headband

A grosgrain ribbon headband is easy to make. And ribbons come in tons of different patterns and colors, so you'll have no trouble making this accessory unique!

What you need:

- a hard plastic headband

- grosgrain ribbon (the same width as the headband)

- scissors

- a hot glue gun (and an adult to help you use it)

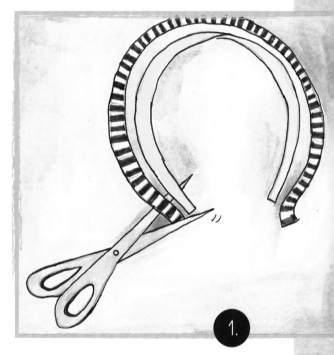

1.

What you do:

1. Lay your ribbon over your headband. Line up one of the ribbon's ends with one end of the headband. Cut the ribbon where it meets the other end of the headband.

2. Warm up your glue gun and get ready to glue! Start at one end of the headband. Put about 2 inches (5 cm) of glue on the headband. Then stick on the ribbon. Make sure the cut end of the ribbon lines up with the end of the headband. Also make sure the ribbon goes on straight.

3. Continue to add 2 inches (5 cm) of glue at a time, pressing the ribbon on top as you go. Pull the ribbon tight. Make sure it lies smoothly. Continue until all the ribbon has been glued onto the top of the headband.

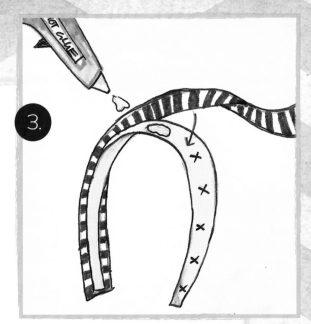

4. At the ends of the headband, the ribbon will be wider than the headband. Put a line of glue along the bottom edge of the headband, starting at one pointed end and going up 1 inch (2.5 cm).

5. Fold in the ends of the ribbon around the side of the headband, sticking the ribbon ends to the glue. Repeat steps 4 and 5 on the other end of the headband.

FOLD ENDS IN

6. You're finished! Just let the glue dry. Then pull your hair back with your new headband for the perfect preppy hairdo.

Your PREPPY Look

Elegant, simple, and clean, preppy fashion never goes out of style. And there are countless ways for you to add your own modern, distinctive touch to the classic staples. You can take this look wherever you want to go with it.

What kind of prep will you be? Will you try Zac Efron's cool and casual approach? Or will you aim for Elle Fanning's preppy chic look? Pick the perfect shirt, pair it with the coolest pants, and check yourself out. Then mix it up and try something completely different. Just remember to make your style your own. And have fun figuring it out!

Button-down shirts and fitted blazers look preppy and feel comfy.

Simple, tasteful dresses belong front and center in your preppy closet.

Loafers, boat shoes, and boots will give you head-to-toe prep style.

Preppy Resources

Do you want to learn more about being preppy? Check out these ideas.

Where to Find Preppy Goodies

- Look online for typical New England-based clothing stores. You'll find a lot of the styles that you probably won't see at your local mall.

- Thrift stores are great for blazers, polo shirts, hats, dresses, and skirts. Look for clothing from the 1950s to the 1980s.

- Go to estate sales, garage sales, and antique stores for interesting jewelry. You might find the perfect pearls or men's watch.

Where to Find Preppy Tutorials and Classes

- Look for hair, makeup, and clothing tutorials on YouTube.

- Read crafting blogs to find ways to make preppy headbands, jewelry, and belts.

- Visit websites or blogs about preppy style icons, like Grace Kelly, Audrey Hepburn, Katherine Hepburn, or Robert Redford. You can also find blogs about the preppy lifestyle.

Songs with a Preppy Vibe

"Oxford Comma" by Vampire Weekend

"Seven" by Dave Matthews Band

"Again" by Bruno Mars

"Hey There Delilah" by Plain White T's

"Bubble Toes" by Jack Johnson

GLOSSARY

cable-knit: made with a knitting stitch that looks like the twist of a cable with two strands

chambray: a light fabric that has a faded denim color

distressed: worn or torn, as with jeans

fedora: a low, soft felt hat with the crown creased lengthwise

grosgrain: a strong, corded fabric used for ribbons

henley: a sweater or shirt that has no collar and a buttoned opening at the neck

iconic: a person or image that becomes a symbol of a style, time period, event, or place

lacrosse: a game in which players get a ball into a goal using a long stick with a mesh net at one end

madras: a light cotton, usually with a plaid pattern

Nantucket Reds: red pants named for an island off the coast of Massachusetts

paisley: a pattern that include distinct shapes that look like curved raindrops

silhouette: the shape of something, such as a dress

SOURCE NOTES

8. Taylor Swift, "Taylor Swift's Style Secrets," *Seventeen*, accessed May 30, 2013, http://www.seventeen.com/entertainment/covers /taylor-swift-style-quotes-8#slide-2.

9. Brantley Bardin, "Man of Style: Zac Efron," *InStyle Australia*, accessed May 30, 2013, http://www.instylemag.com.au/Article /Special-Offers/Inside-InStyle/Man-of-Style-Zac-Efron.

10. Eva Chen, "Elle Fanning Models Summer Braids by Didier Malige," *TeenVogue*, May 30, 2013, http://www.teenvogue.com/beauty/hair/2011-05/elle-fanning-hair/?intro.

FURTHER INFORMATION

Shoket, Ann. *Seventeen Ultimate Guide to Style: How to Find Your Perfect Look.* **Philadelphia: Running Press, 2011.**
Not sure if classic preppy or another style is best for you? Then look to this helpful book to guide you!

Teen Vogue
http://www.teenvogue.com
Check out this site for the latest in preppy and other fashion styles.

Thomas, Isabel. *Being a Fashion Stylist.* **Minneapolis: Lerner Publications, 2013.**
Ever wondered what it's like to work as a fashion stylist? This book is the perfect find for aspiring fashionistas!

Walker, Jackie. *Expressionista: How to Express Your True Self Through (and Despite) Fashion.* **New York: Aladdin, 2013.**
This title will help you discover your fashion persona and set up a closet to reflect your sense of style.

INDEX

PHOTO ACKNOWLEDGMENTS

The images in this book are used with the permission of: © Olga Kudryashova/Shutterstock, p. 3; © Buso23/Bigstock, p. 4 (top); © Anton Oparin/Shutterstock, pp. 4 (bottom), 14 (middle left & bottom), 17 (middle left & bottom left), 24 (top & bottom), 30 (middle & bottom right), 33 (top left), 42 (right), 43 (top right & center); © Ugo Cutilli/Shutterstock, pp. 5 (top), 24 (middle), 48; © Wanchai/Shutterstock, pp. 5 (bottom), 33 (middle right); © Karkas/Bigstock, pp. 5 (bottom), 16 (top middle & bottom right); © Odd Anderson/AFP/Getty Images, p. 6 (left); © Miriam May/Getty Images, p. 6 (right); © Chip Somodevilla/Getty Images, p. 7 (top); © Jaguar PS/Shutterstock, pp. 7 (bottom left), 10 (bottom left), 38 (middle); © S_bukley/Shutterstock, pp. 7 (bottom middle), 8 (top), 12 (top); © Mike Zarrilli/Getty Images, p. 7 (bottom right); © Featureflash/Shutterstock, pp. 8 (bottom left & bottom right), 9 (top), 38 (top left), 39 (top left); © Scott Prokop/Shutterstock, p. 8 (bottom middle); © Paul Smith/Featureflash/Shutterstock, pp. 9 (middle), 16 (bottom middle), 27 (bottom middle); © Allan Grant/Time & Life Pictures/Getty Images, p. 9 (bottom); © Kathclick/Bigstock, pp. 10 (top), 37 (top left); © Henry Harris/Featureflash/Shutterstock, pp. 10 (bottom right), 19 (bottom right); © Kurniawan1972/Dreamstime, p. 11 (right); © Steve Vas/Featureflash/Shutterstock, pp. 11 (left), 17 (middle right), 19 (top left); © Michaeljung/Shutterstock, p. 12 (left); © Nata Sha/Shutterstock, pp. 12 (bottom right), 16 (top right), 17 (bottom right), 18 (bottom left), 21 (all), 33 (bottom right), 37 (top right), 39 (bottom right), 43 (bottom left & bottom right); © Jupiterimages/Botanica/Getty Images, p. 13 (top left); © Catwalker/Shutterstock, pp. 13 (top right), 42 (left), 43 (top left); © Ondine32/E+/Getty Images, p. 13 (bottom left); © Gordana Sermek/Shutterstock, p. 13 (bottom right); © Ovidiu Hrubaru/Shutterstock, p. 14 (top left); © Champiofoto/Shutterstock, p. 14 (top right); © Lev Radin/Shutterstock, p. 15 (top left); © Giliane Mansfeldt/Independent Picture Service, pp. 15 (top right & middle right), 16 (bottom left), 17 (top), 18 (bottom right), 25 (bottom right), 33 (bottom middle); © iStockphoto/Thinkstock, p. 15 (bottom left); © Forgiss/Bigstock, p. 15 (bottom right); © Debby Wong/Shutterstock, pp. 16 (top left), 38 (bottom right); © Lalouetto/Bigstock, p. 18 (top left); © solominviktor/Shutterstock, p. 18 (top right); © K2 images/Shutterstock, p. 19 (top right); © Crystalfoto/Shutterstock, p. 19 (bottom left); © Mnowicki/Shutterstock, p. 20; © iStockphoto/mypokcik, p. 25 (bottom left); © Nickolay Rudenko/Dreamstime, p. 25 (top); © Gromovataya/Shutterstock, p. 26 (top left); © Bernashafo/Shutterstock, p. 26 (middle bottom); © Allan Bregg/Shutterstock, p. 26 (bottom); © Elnur/Bigstock, p. 26 (top right & middle top); © Gpointstudio/Shutterstock, p. 27 (top); © South12th Photography/Shutterstock, p. 27 (bottom left); © Ewilkerson/Dreamstime, p. 27 (bottom right); © TrotzOlga/Shutterstock, p. 30 (top); © c12/Shutterstock, p. 30 (bottom left); © Cosmin Munteanu/Shutterstock, p. 31 (top right); © Anklav/Shutterstock, p. 31 (top left); © S.Dashkevych/Shutterstock, p. 31 (middle right); © Dean Bertoncelj/Shutterstock, p. 31 (bottom right); © iStockphoto/wakila, p. 31 (bottom left); © Robertlang/Bigstock, p. 31 (middle left); © Pamela Mullins/Shutterstock, p. 32 (top); © iStockphoto/eliferen, p. 32 (middle left); © Nito/Shutterstock, p. 32 (middle right); © Warren Goldswain/Shutterstock, p. 32 (bottom); © Daria Minaeva/Shutterstock, p. 33 (top right); © New vave/Shutterstock, p. 33 (bottom left); © Alexandra Lande/Shutterstock, p. 36 (top left); © Baibaz/Shutterstock, p. 36 (top middle & top right);© Serg Zastavkin/Shutterstock, p. 36 (bottom); © Caroline Purser/Photographer's Choice/Getty Images, p. 37 (bottom left); © Helga Esteb/Shutterstock, p. 37 (bottom right); © Takayuki/Shutterstock, p. 38 (top right); © Matusciac Alexandru/Shutterstock, p. 38 (bottom left); © Joana Lopes/Shutterstock, p. 39 (top right); © 41/Shutterstock, p. 39 (bottom left).

Backgrounds: © 00798/Shutterstock, pp. 1, 4–5, 6–7; © Togataki/Shutterstock, pp. 2, 8–9, 10, 11, 27, 28–29, 32, 39, 40–41, 42–43, 44–45, 46–47, 48; © gnoma/Shutterstock, p. 15; © SongPixels/Shutterstock, pp. 22–23; © Anatoly Tiplyashin/Shutterstock, pp. 30–31; © N_ZHM/Shutterstock, p. 34–35.

Front cover: © Togataki/Shutterstock (stencil art background); © 00798/Shutterstock (vintage pattern); © nito/Shutterstock (fedora hat); © Karkas/Shutterstock (skirt); © Bernashafo/Shutterstock (shoes); © Dean Bertoncelj/Shutterstock (charm bracelet); © TrotzOlga/Shutterstock (headband); © Lalouetto/Bigstock (jacket); © buso23/Bigstock (pearls); © S.Dashkevych/Shutterstock (wrist watch); © Giliane Mansfeldt/Independent Picture Service (blue shirt).

Back cover: © 00798/Shutterstock (vintage pattern); © wanchai/Shutterstock (red bag); © Giliane Mansfeldt/Independent Picture Service (shoes).